Pachuco Skull with Sombrero
Los Angeles, 1970

Lawrence Welsh

Unlikely Books
www.UnlikelyStories.org
New Orleans, Louisiana

Unlikely Books
www.UnlikelyStories.org
New Orleans, Louisiana

Preface by Belinda Subraman

He doesn't separate himself from the land
where his word rodeo comes alive.
"o god if we move
and talk like birds
say the whippoorwill
and desert wren"

No gecko scuttles in front of him without notice
on a cosmic cellular level.
"how the poor and broken
how their faces
grieve again
and long for some touch
like the wood for a coming
cross or coffin"

His desert sun is always glaring
spotlighting his perceptions.
"when arrivals leave
from other rooms
i realize she's gone
with only a scream now
for her own
for my own
new beginning"

At his best he's like the arid land
bringing life, to words, against all odds.
"until all i see
is sun and light
sun and light
and pray for
a moving on"

His memories are maps to everywhere.
"those who feel
the steel
recognize those
who touch
immortality
are that much closer
to home"

Warm breezes swirl with metaphors.
"almost ash in the desert:
the relentless sun
and stillness of wind
and no wind."

He spits errant grit from his dust blown mouth
"let us know
without knowing
let amputations or sullen disease
revolve and become
a universal occurrence
and a universal kiss"

and continues walking to his destination.
"that only owls
        mesa wolves
and coyotes may see."

His writing's deepest beauty is connection.

The Order in Which They Appear

Pachuco Skull with Sombrero
Los Angeles, 1970

Pachuco Skull with Sombrero:
Los Angeles, 1970

freeways to bones
and then again
the spray-painted image
around atwater, echo park
becomes all drivers
as testament
where one can own
any dream
towards pasadena
or griffith park turnoffs
that mumble a local's song:
our lady of the angels
our skulls at st. vibiana
the st. joe's fiesta
of spinning wheels
and every word a memory
of fitting in.
let us pass
in quickness or fly over
concrete and lanes
and think about who became
who remains stamped
by the blood
by the shots
on the streets
we knew
we owned as home

Rio Grande Roadrunner

forgive eyes
that become mexico
or the border patrol's
glassed intent beyond
the water.
out here
all appearances
disappearances
can whisper
or shout:
i am the line
an escapee
of the blue sky
desert air
and fall or rise
for some resurrection
like a new palette
or canvas cleansed
by the freedom
of a scrubbing
of a washing
the taunts of some
to jump
to rush
to complete a loca's
or local's dare

Dust and Fair

a dozen sheffield knives
for the wheel of death
with yvonne
the beautiful yvonne
from the mescalero apache nation
married to the rhinestone roper
for ceremonies to endure
like the puma woman on a bed of nails
(no meow now)
or the fire eating sword swallower
blowing chupacabra smoke
on the lizard boy.
what day once they leave
only the dust knows
to rise and settle
like a grave
like the whispers of over
like callings from the sky
from the clouds
like the maps
like the directions full
of faulty and guiding stars
like a phone call that hangs up
only a ringtone
for the memories of home

Gold Mountain/Black Crow

one frozen shot believes
to still
for december
or memories of colors
like hallucinations
that stop
in freeze frame and say
this is like a minor fire
all lit up
and continuing to burn

After the West Texas Dust Up

let the used
like a '64 impala
know a bloodshot ford
or the '67 cougar
to become a sound once again
like a soundtrack
like wayne "the train" hancock
from dallas
singing "juke joint jumpin'"
and "thunderstorms and neon signs"
and then drive off in pairs
in a '42 ford
the 1950 desoto woody
will know only silence
by midnight
and the lot
only yucca trails
only the chaparrals' whistle
only the absences and memory
by far

Compressor Jack

hell house
hit
haltingly
hoping the word
would suffice

old shotgun shack
can move
its foundation
slip back
to the fifth ward —
a smaller street
a shorter stay
a means
of stripping down

South Central Driver, 1968

After Robert Kennedy, RIP

endlessness on normandie
endlessness on vermont
endlessness on budlong
has ended now
at the ambassador
in our living room
(old black and white zenith)
that murders the city.
all brakes now for the killing
the shots
the spirit of the hearse
might give our neighborhood walkers
the breath
the water
the blood
the reasons
to never believe again

Old Sunland Adobe

board up
wire up
bar up
sun up
becomes plaster
to conceal what was
only ghosts now
of the river
like dry bed rio grande
to flow once june
comes around
and then the yellow winged
black bird
to perch
like a person
says you won't find
the flood gate
the caskets
you will become
only a seeker
on sunland's floor

Eagle Pipe Carrier

in grave's essence
to see hallucination's visions
some wonder
how it came to be soft
pliable from minnesota
or not at all.
forgive the landscape
and the years
the missing buffalo
the fights that left nothing
and remember that to forget
is impossible
almost like ignoring names
or the words
almost impossible to recall
to suggest
and light it finally
with pow wow blend
and say a prayer
for the ones before
for the memories now
and those that never were
but are forever rising

Rio Grande Vulture

memory paints black and grey
amongst the brown dust story
or storm becomes a waking
to the new water.
put me in the carnival
and let me spin to fly
and say good enough
for a sending
for a flying off
to only new sand
and eventual desert stars

Sustained Harmonic Drone

a ticking to hit
     click
     like a ball
     railroad standard
pocket watch
     from cleveland
ohio
     and pianos—
ghost wurlitzers
smashed with chairs
     pool cues
          and burnt:
listen to the ash
the blackened wood:
     it sings
     it sings

North Jazz

for stops in resonance
in refrain
remake a life too backwards
say in snow
those gentle arms
to hold and freeze
by the sea
and let go
like cranes and egrets
some vision of flying
and dying in white

Under the Pier #2

essence grinds essence
like sand hidden becomes
green glass like mickeys
or guinness and schlitz malt liquor
are good for you to cheer
a local's song like a jig or reel
that plays amongst the darkness
and the crashing waves
and turns and turns to pacific stones
and turns to an unreachable end
that grieves in penance
in permanence for a coming
and going on again

John L. Sullivan, Irish Bourbon Whiskey, Bardstown, Kentucky

whose legacy is good enough
to fire off like a right, left, right
and then again some alley collapse
becomes all smashed glass
like flawed jewels we pick up
to cut our hands, our arms
and bleed out for destinies
stilled and given
before we were born?

go on, go on and take it
use it, pour it on:
it's a vestige of never over coming
of becoming all and the same
all and the same
to hit again finally
and raise our eyes
above a floating canvas
above a collapsing floor

Blood Moon Rise:
Santa Teresa

and all the silver
turns slightly off
until stones
      yucca
            ocotillo
and honey mesquite
blows holes in realization's reality
of a darkened hue:
bury me or let my ashes go
become the place
that i am
become the place of a piercing
that flows
with a crucifixion
that only owls
      mesa wolves
and coyotes may see

The Broken Statuary

a losing to become
say one or the other
in a dream
or some testament:
mother dead
in a fisherman's sweater
this time not smiling
or grieving
or st. francis
almost ash in the desert:
the relentless sun
and stillness of wind
and no wind.
let us know
without knowing
let amputations or sullen disease
revolve and become
a universal occurrence
and a universal kiss

Steel Reserve/Alloy Series/Hard Pineapple

let one sip
become a final note
or taste of oblivion
on the tracks
where we hide vestiges
of what we were:
young once
with a future
old once
to pronounce:
those who feel
the steel
recognize those
who touch
immortality
are that much closer
to home

The Dorothy Day/Thomas Merton Correspondence

how the poor and broken
how their faces
grieve again
and long for some touch
like the wood for a coming
cross or coffin
the crucifixion would guarantee
at least the end:
an opening psalm
and testament
the beginning
to a lasting lectionary
or the final hum
of an echoing refrain

The Outlaw Trail

say st. john
away from topeka
witchita
and all remembered
in an oldsmobile
or buick roadmaster
that got you there.
say illinois or pueblo
some night
and dream
dream of sleep
but it never comes.
and pray then simply
pray with the flash
of gunfire
the green rosary
the lowering down
to rise and say
i remember
or sense it out
it flows westward
it becomes a beginning
and end frozen
in this
or another's
unraveling time
and memory

Begging for Vultures #2

only bones one day
or face down
and not moving
tomorrow
to only let
the desert take over
here
until all i see
is sun and light
sun and light
and pray for
a moving on
only naturally
to a crash
and crash again
with no hope
for a getting
or staggering up

Last Rites

measure the amounts now
for a journey
and let them go peacefully
with no belief
or all belief
in this is at least
a way
a carrying over
with no carrying
needed at all

Blood or Whiskey

cage it for a spell
if possible
or not at all to ramble
for something new:
cavan or dublin
nenagh or limerick
and a step off down
to the pit
and around the base
for a thirst:
we will become
demonstrations for its way:
and never know
or someday when
enough is enough again

After the Old Crow Medicine Show

as nashville now
as runner before
to start or back
to the hills
to become
what nobody wanted:
a fiddle and banjo
the slam of a
green guitar
and on again
to the rails
the simplest ones
with all directions to turn

Minneapolis Trees in April

some spring never comes
only winter to wait out
an eternity as such
where no branches begin to bud
only the freeze like snow
or the whisper of last year's still ice
or iced monographs
called may's presence
or june's final reprieve

Boston Snow

engage some aspect of it for days now—
the falling as primitive white
to smooth out any chance
of the uses outdoors

*

some said dorchester or back bay
but what can one own in a week—
the wildness of southie or what exists anymore?
perhaps a trek out
then after the fall
the knowledge of this: one time
and then again: no more
no more

Uil/Sligo

rising sun flag
is fenian bound
for stashed underground
as picture perfect:

> *harp*
> *wolfhound*
> *celtic cross*

will lead them on
even when hidden
for symbols will
get them killed
and sold
100 years later
for 100,000 pounds
in a shining
dublin auction house.
for one family buried
from cork
then flew it
again freely
by the irish sea

The Death Room

for whose crucifix
remained grasped
w/ anointer's oil
at the foot
of tomorrow's sorrow?

and who rides
bicycle's picture
of ballycommon
or a sister now
at violet bank?

when arrivals leave
from other rooms
i realize she's gone
with only a scream now
for her own
for my own
new beginning

A Wake at Richmond

clay pipes
she said
and poteen
and her father's
pocket crucifix
would remember
what needed telling:
stories
for the dead man
like a nenagh youth
or tales of leaving
(all who did)
to america or australia.
he became only
her internalization
of hours
and hours with the
dead man's rosary
and memories
and the passing
of artifacts
and her guiding
them home

For the Hung Irish

for they after
deserved a recitation
or note
dragging on the floor
like a map
and then slammed
inside
an unmarked grave
that gives
no names
not even a
simple spectacle
for the living

Franciscan Prayers

in the moment
of absolutes
let us recall
a field
east of
holy cross road
and south of
the organ mountains
that gives only
grey and black lights
and remember where
the pecan trees stood
for some permanence
that's at least known
perhaps painted
and forgotten again
and stilled
in death
as a fragment
of dying
and living only
on memories

Otra Negro

the remembrance is a killer
on the mountain
or mountain killer
leaning backwards
for sundown's again now
begin in purchase
of others and how
they became a city
like cornered in juarez
or the rough stoppage
on a dead end street
like this is your other
this is the price of looking
of behaving in a rational
and irrational way

Ghost Girlfriends

malt liquor
and angel dust

i knew to
forget them

and now they are
questions

a few faces
like abstractions

or maybe my soul
craves a beginning

and gone
to the blank slates

they're blank
no more

Portugal

in the sand
        silence
the lovers said
        "a fish"
or "sandeman el porto"
for black velvet

        capes

they had a room
for pennies
and blank pages
to fill
with novels still
unread
or in
        process:

        lowry
        hemingway

and a casting out
for lovers –
the final release
the moving on then
by the door

Bottom City

perhaps in the hills
behind the whisky a go go
or 6th and wall at crabby joe's
or the fresh corn tortillas
at la parilla on brooklyn and chicago
or hawthorne's eastside lager on tap

*

let western avenue
drop us in south central
at von's market
and the silver dollar liquor boutique
on manchester will soften us
dim the lights until the riots
the earthquakes
and the hope for a train out
barreling through
to another town

The Sheiks of Shake, 1978

harmonicas are mirrors
to santa monica boulevard
and venice sunsets:

all blood red
for spilling all
southern california dreams
become a chance
and then again
a tale
like some blues
like cross harp
twice removed
and spat out
from the stars again

High Mountain Spirit Dancers

after the mescalero apache

el paso's blood moon
is stoned in circles
going round for the land
for the reverb
for painted rocks
of 1,000 shades
of brown
and gone again
for leather on dust
for bells and the clank
of wood headdresses.
o god if we move
and talk like birds
say the whippoorwill
and desert wren
will we find
the speed to move
like one shot of crystal
up a nostril
or the hit of dust
in a lung
with eyes alert
and fragmented our brains
and souls only wanting more
but more is a cedar fire
and the drum
the propulsion to keep going
in a circle
like dust devils
with no control
for a rising up

The Drinking Game #2

a loser wins in retrospect
and plays dominoes at the track
to watch and say some incompletion ends
with a derby spring round
to aluminum and glass
like cherry miller or lime chelada
in gold buckets we take
and mount our dreams
on impossibilities that carry us
across and outside the lines
and lets us be only possible stars
of this passing
of this only taste for the wheels
of a given and giving town
that drinks every thirst away

The Carousel Rider

let mothers
hold brass

and stand for
the black horse's

smile is golden
to forever make

circles and circles
a permanent home.

and brown eyes
for her

daughter's disbelief
of this is life

this will be
only it

and so
much more

After Blues Jumped the Rabbit

some teeth are better than none
or skinned in colorado but where?
grand junction, gunnison, greeley or fort collins
to drape over a blue canyon
that sings like a dobro or martin steel string
for a summer in a peterbuilt or kenworth
becomes those gone on with only hides
or skins left behind

The Sweet Science

now they're all knocked out
even in inglewood
or south central's rabbit punches
i never saw coming
and lace up everlast gloves

my father said you will learn
you will battle to survive
and learn the sweet science
as sometimes in a haze
in numbness
in remembrance
they tell me you were crazy
you didn't back up
crazy white boy from south central
and who showed you that
certainly not canvas back hogan
or another that returns only losses
from a lost country

look father
look dad
you gave me everything now
and i'm still throwing punches at shadows
until the ghosts are only memories
of another's escape

Born and raised in South Central Los Angeles, **Lawrence Welsh** lives in El Paso, Texas. A first generation Irish American and award-winning journalist, Welsh has published eleven books of poetry, including *Begging for Vultures: New and Selected Poems, 1994-2009* (University of New Mexico Press). Now in a second printing, this collection won the New Mexico-Arizona Book Award. It was also named a Notable Book by Southwest Books of the Year and a finalist for both the PEN Southwest Book Award and the Writers' League of Texas Book Award.

In 2011, *Irish America* magazine in New York City named him one of the "Top 100 Irish Americans" of the year. In 1987, he received The Society of Professional Journalists/Sigma Delta Chi Outstanding Graduating Journalist Award from California State University, Long Beach. In 1979, he co-founded The Alcoholics, the L.A. punk rock band. As part of its Punk Archive Series, Sahlugg Records of Los Angeles in 2017 released *East of Sepulveda: 1979-1982*, a retrospective of the band's studio and live cuts.

A winner of the Bardsong Press Celtic Voice Writing Award in Poetry and the 2017 *Pen World* magazine Montegrappa essay competition, Welsh is an English professor at El Paso Community College. His poetry, fiction, reviews, essays, as well as journalistic writings, have appeared in more than 200 national and regional magazines, journals, newspapers and anthologies, including *Puerto del Sol, Hawaii Review, The Louisiana Review, Rio Grande Review, The Texas Observer, The Santa Fe New Mexican, The Irish Echo, Irish America, New Madrid Review, The Wormwood Review, Onthebus, Pearl, Poetry Now, Big Bridge, The Café Review, Nexus, Chiron Review, Poetry Motel, Main Street Rag, The Raven Chronicles, Unlikely Stories, The Powhatan Review, Pitchfork* and the Los Angeles *Daily Breeze,* the 2015 Pulitzer Prize winning newspaper where he spent five years as a reporter and staff writer in the 1980s.

Other Titles by Lawrence Welsh

*Cutting the Wire: Photographs and Poetry from the U.S.-
    Mexico Border* (with Ray Gonzalez and Bruce Berman),
    University of New Mexico Press, (forthcoming)

The Ballad of Slim Angel, Mouthfeel Press, 2017

Blood in the Mix (with John Macker), Lummox Press, 2015

Begging for Vultures: New and Selected Poems, 1994-2009,
    University of New Mexico Press, 2011 (second printing)

Lawrence Welsh Reads, Vox Audio, 2011 (CD)

Carney Takedown, Unlikely Books, 2010

Todd Moore and Lawrence Welsh Read at Acequia Booksellers,
    Vox Audio, 2009 (CD)

Skull Highway, La Alameda Press, 2008

Walking Backwards to Santa Fe, Pitchfork Press, 2007

Believing in Bonfires, Pitchfork Press, 2003

New Shouts at Broken Dreams, Lummox Press, 2001

Rusted Steel and Bordertown Starts, Sundance Press, 1999

Lenny Bruce in El Paso, Non Compos Mentis Press, 1997

Recent Titles from Unlikely Books

www.ingramcontent.com/pod-product-compliance
Lightning Source LLC
Chambersburg PA
CBHW032103040426
42449CB00007B/1167